The Three Wishes

Retold by Lesley Sims

Illustrated by Elisa Squillace

Reading Consultant: Alison Kelly
Roehampton University

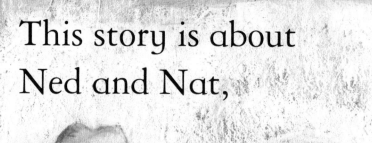

This story is about
Ned and Nat,

a fairy

and a sausage.

Ned and Nat were
hungry.

They were
always hungry.

5

Ned worked in
the fields.

One day, he helped
a fairy.

"Thank you. Have three wishes," said the fairy.

Ned ran home.

"Nat! We have three wishes!" he shouted.

"Ooh!" said Nat.
"I wish for..."

"A sausage!" said Ned.

Ned was cross.

"I wish the sausage was on the end of your nose!"

And it was.

Nat was
very,
very,
very cross.

"Oops!" said Ned.

"Ned!" wailed Nat.
"Do something!"

"I wish the sausage was off your nose," said Ned.

And it was.

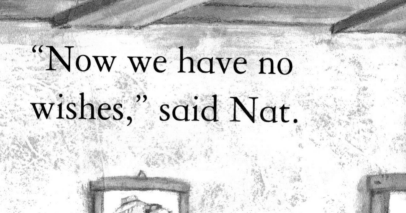

"Now we have no wishes," said Nat.

24

"But we do have a sausage!" said Ned.

PUZZLES

Puzzle 1

Can you help Ned and the fairy spot the differences? There are 6 to find.

Puzzle 2

Can you put the pictures
in the right order?

A  B

C

D  E

Puzzle 3

Match the words to the picture.

plate Ned table Nat cup

mouse sausage sunflower

Answers to puzzles

Puzzle 1

Puzzle 2

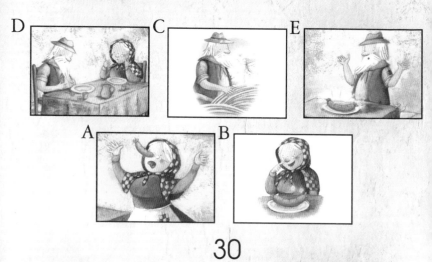

Puzzle 3

Nat · Ned · sunflower

plate

plate

mouse · table · cup · sausage

About The Three Wishes

The Three Wishes is an old folk tale from Northern Europe. This version is adapted from the tale told in Sweden.

Designed by Sam Chandler
Series designer: Russell Punter

First published in 2009 by Usborne Publishing Ltd., Usborne House,
83-85 Saffron Hill, London EC1N 8RT, England. www.usborne.com
Copyright © 2009 Usborne Publishing Ltd.